YOUNG SERVER'S
Book of the Mass

Kenneth Guentert

Resource Publications, Inc.
San Jose, California

Editorial director: Kenneth Guentert
Editor: Nick Wagner
Managing editor: Elizabeth J. Asborno
Cover design and production: Ron Niewald
Illustrations: Stan Bomgarden

Reprint Department
Resource Publications, Inc.
160 E. Virginia Street #290
San Jose, CA 95112-5876

Library of Congress Cataloging in Publication Data available.

ISBN 0-89390-078-8

Printed in the United States of America

99 98 97 96 95 | 8 7 6 5 4

CONTENTS

TO MINISTRY COORDINATORS

As you may know, many liturgists think that ministry of altar service belongs properly to adults and not to children.

Without getting into the merits of adult servers, which are considerable, I think that child servers are staying around principally because people have a sneaking suspicion that there is no better catechesis than getting children into the thick of things.

I know that was true of myself, thirty years ago, and I don't know why it should be any different now.

Certainly, things have changed for servers. They don't have Latin to learn and do not have as much to do—the latter phenomenon coming mostly I think because no one has really studied the ministry in light of the significant changes the church has implemented since Vatican II. Before I wrote this book, I looked at the available training aids for altar servers and all seem to be similar to what I was trained with thirty years ago, updated to accommodate the missing Latin and the moved furniture.

Yet more has changed than the placement of our furniture. Thirty years ago, serving was exciting because I was privy to action the assembly was not. That has changed. The altar servers are back in the assembly (along with the priest, I might add), much less visible, and not at all unique in their ministerial role.

What have not changed, though, are the servers themselves. Young servers still like action more than sitting still and, with the attention span of gnats, are open to the wonderful distractions of the environment. During the canon, which seemed to go on for days when I was a server, I would get lost in thought about the bells, the Last Supper icon in front of me, the golden vessels, the Latin. During the eucharistic prayer, which passes no less slowly for children today, young servers can let the words wash over them and wonder about our mysteries. The Altar. The Cup. The Bread. The Garments. It is indeed a perfect time for catechesis.

So I wrote this book, not so much to tell altar servers how to behave (though I do some of that), but to answer questions about what is out there in front of them and even to raise some possibilities for their wandering minds.

The Young Server's Book of the Mass presents sophisticated liturgical information in the language of young people. Which is to say, it is concrete, colorful, direct, and open to the distraction which is not a distraction. For example, I include fish in the menu of liturgical foods because it is there in our earliest eucharistic stories and because young people like fish stories. And I asked my friend and teacher Stan Bomgarden to supply his vintage cartoons, which manage to be both biblical and whimsical at the same time.

Despite this playfulness, the book has the utterly serious purpose of trying to give young people some sense of "the holy"— especially as it relates to our worship. Indeed, that is the motif of the book. If young people can learn that their role is special (i.e., holy), style and grace will follow. Even if it takes thirty years.

*** *

Special thanks go to Leo Keegan, who criticized an early draft and loaned me a treasured and musty copy of *The Catholic Picture Dictionary* (Duell, Sloan, and Pearce, 1948); Bill Freburger, who proofed my first draft and prevented a number of embarrassing errors; Stan Bomgarden, my biblical mentor; and Larry Johnson, whose *Word and Eucharist Handbook* (Resource Publications, Inc. 1986) was my main reference.

YOUNG SERVER'S
Book of the Mass

Book of the Most

HOLY

In this book, I'll often use the word "holy." This does not mean "good" or "nice" or "better than" or "like an angel." In Hebrew, the word *kodesh* means "holy" in the sense of "set aside" or "special." You are special because you are a server.

NORMAL   ABNORMAL   HOLY

A HOLY PEOPLE

You are part of a "holy people." This does not mean you are better than people who do not go to your church or who do not believe in your God. It means you are part of a special community, one special to God, with special responsibilities to make the world a better place.

As a server, you are "holy" in another way. You have a special role to play— helping the priest, especially, and showing other members of the assembly how to behave.

You will notice that other people have special (holy) roles too:

The assembly, which sings, and listens, and prays. The assembly has the most important role. Without people, there is no one to worship God.

The cross-bearer, who carries the cross and leads the minister or people in procession. You might fill this role.

The torch-bearer, who carries a candle in processions. You might fill this role.

The **lector**, who reads from the Bible.

The communion minister, who helps to distribute the consecrated bread and wine, both to members of the assembly and to members of the community who are sick or otherwise unable to come to church.

The usher (or minister of hospitality), who welcomes people as they come in, helps them find seats, and takes up the collection.

The gift bearer, who brings up the gifts at the Presentation of Gifts and sometimes prepares the altar table for the celebration.

The musician, who helps the assembly pray with music.

The deacon, who assists the presider and sometimes gives the homily.

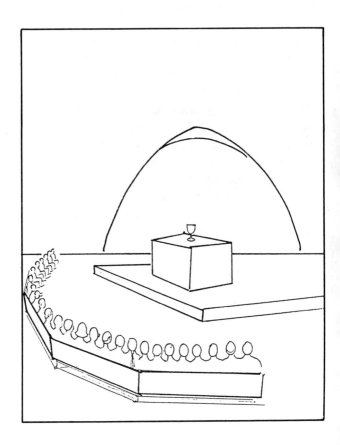

A HOLY PEOPLE

The homilist, who preaches and comments on the Scripture readings. (Often, the homilist and presider are the same person.)

The presider is the priest who leads the liturgy and leads the assembly in prayer.

In addition, many other people behind the scenes make the Mass happen in a special way. There are **planners**, who plan the Sunday service weeks and sometimes months in advance; **artists**, who created the space you worship in and who decorate it from week to week with special banners, plants, and symbols; and **catechists**, who prepare candidates for the sacraments that might be celebrated at a Mass.

So every Sunday Mass is a special (holy) event.

HOLY TIMES

The entire Christian community gathers for worship at special times. The most special time for gathering is Sunday, which is the day that Jesus rose from the dead. So every Sunday, we remember Jesus' death and resurrection.

There are other days of the year when the entire assembly tries to gather for worship. In the United States, these days are:

- The Assumption of Mary (August 15)

- All Saints (November 1)

- The Immaculate Conception of Mary (December 8)

- Christmas (December 25)

- The Solemnity of Mary, the Mother of God (New Year's Day)

- The Ascension of Our Lord (a Thursday, forty days after Easter Sunday)

These days are special to the United States and are called—can you guess?—holy days.

The *most special week of the year*—here we go again—is called Holy Week, which includes Passion Sunday, Holy Thursday, Good Friday, and Holy Saturday.

The *most special time of the year* is a three-day feast called the Easter Triduum (after the Latin for "three-day"). Easter Triduum is one feast made up of three days beginning on Holy Thursday evening and ending on Easter Sunday evening.

Easter, in the eyes of the church, is not one day but fifty! It begins with the Triduum and lasts until Pentecost Sunday, seven weeks later.

HOLY TIMES

The church is like the earth—it has its own seasons. Most of the year is called Ordinary Time because it's, well, ordinary, like most of the time. In between are the "extraordinary" times like Advent (four weeks), Christmas (several weeks), Lent (six weeks), and Easter (seven weeks). Each of these seasons has a different color and a different feeling about it—just as spring, summer, fall, and winter have their own moods and colors and special activities.

HOLY PLACE

Most assemblies set aside a special place to gather for worship. In olden times, people might have called such a place a "temple." We call it a "church," which is another word for "assembly."

Your church, no matter how different is is from churches in the next town, will have things in common with the temple where the Israelites worshiped God. For example:

The Tabernacle: This was God's home. In Moses' time, it was a large tent. No human, except for the high priest, even went into this tent—and he only went once a year. In our time,

13

the tabernacle is a much smaller place where we keep the bread that has become the body of Christ. It looks a little like a cupboard, but it is really a shelter for God. When I was an alter server, the tabernacle was part of the altar. Now it is often set away from the altar in a more quiet area.

The Altar: In Moses' time, the altar was very much like a barbecue. Really. Officially, it was called "an altar of holocaust," but that is fancy talk for a place where you cook meat. So why did the temple have a barbecue? You have to understand that for ancient people food was very important (that much should not be hard to understand). They believed that if they gave God some of their crop or flocks or herds—especially before they took anything for themselves— God would bless them with more food than they needed. So how do you give food to God? One way is to destroy the animal—by burning it—which is like sending it to another world. In later years, the priests kept these "holy sacrifices" for themselves and ate them. That was another way of getting the offering to God.

The altar in your church comes from that very same altar of holocaust. The cube-shaped altar in my church even looks like one of these ancient altars. Of course, we don't burn anything there, but we still use the ancient language: "Lamb of God, who take away the sin of the world...." At Passover, the angel of death "passed over" every house that had lamb's blood sprinkled on the doorway. The Israelites, therefore, would kill a lamb at Passover, burn, and eat it as a way of remembering how they were saved from death. For us, the lamb of God is Christ and we remember how we were saved from death at every Mass.

Altars of holocaust were made of stone. Older altars in Catholic churches contain a stone with bone fragments from Christian martyrs. This is a concrete (pun intended) way of reminding you that this is indeed an altar of sacrifice. Ask your priest if your altar has an altar stone.

The Table: In Moses' time, this was a piece of furniture that held the "bread of the Presence"—holy bread that was offered to God. In our churches, we place the bread on the altar—which is why the altar is sometimes also called "the table of the Lord" or an "altar table." It is really two pieces of furniture in one.

Lamp of God: A lamp burned outside the tabernacle in the Israelite temple to show that God was inside his "house." In your church, you can find a lamp burning all the time to show that God is here too.

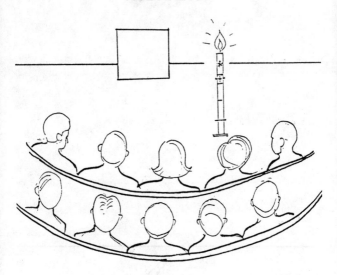

During the Easter season, look also for the Easter candle. It is there to remind you of Christ, the light of the world, and it is lit only when the assembly gather for worship. Can you guess why?

HOLY PLACE

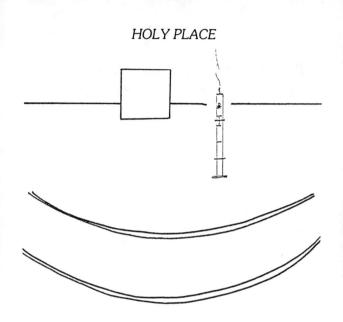

(Turn page for answer.)

Because after resurrection, Christ lives in the people. If the people go out, the lamp goes out.

HOLY STORIES

Our Mass really comes from many stories about Jesus (and others). Here are two:

Story One: Jesus went up into the hills, and sat down there. Great crowds came to him, bringing with them the lame, the blind, the dumb, and many others, and they put them at his feet, and he healed them. Jesus called his students together and said, "I am concerned about this crowd because they have been with me for three days and have had nothing to eat. I am afraid to send them away because they might get faint." His students said, "We're in the desert. Where can we get enough food to feed them?"

Jesus said, "How much bread do you have?"

They said, "Seven loaves, and a few fish."

Jesus told the crowds to sit down. *He took the seven loaves and the fish, and having given thanks, he broke them and gave them to his students, who gave them to the crowd.* And they all ate and were satisfied; and they took up seven baskets full of the broken pieces left over.

Those who ate were four thousand men, not counting women and children (Mt 15:29-38).

Story Two: Now as they were eating the Passover, Jesus *took bread, and blessed it, and broke it, and gave it* to his students and said, "Take, eat; this is my body." *And he took a cup, and when he had given thanks he gave it to them and they all drank from it.* And he said to them, "This is my blood of my covenant, which is poured out for many. Truly, I say to you, I shall not drink again of the fruit of the vine until that day when I drink it new in the kingdom of God" (Mk 14:22-25).

HOLY STORIES

What do the stories have in common?

(Turn page for answer.)

If you said, "They each show Jesus taking bread, blessing it, breaking it, and giving it to his friends," you are right.

How are the two stories different from each other?

(Turn page for answer.)

If you said, "The first story is about bread and fish, and the second story is about bread and wine," you are right.

Fortunately, we take our Mass from the second story; otherwise we might be eating bread and sardines on Sunday morning!

But really the two stories are almost the same. What is important is taking up the food or drink, blessing God for giving us these good things, breaking the bread and pouring out the wine, and then sharing them with our friends.

Can you name the four important actions?

1. Taking up the bread and wine

2. Blessing God for the gifts

3. Breaking the bread, pouring out the wine

4. Giving the bread and wine to friends

It is important to know the four actions because the Mass, really, consists of the same four parts. The four parts have fancy names, but they are the same four actions.

1. Preparation of the Gifts (taking up bread and wine)

2. Eucharistic Prayer (blessing God)

3. Fraction Rite (breaking bread/pouring out wine)

4. Communion (sharing bread and wine)

Can you recognize these four parts of the Mass?

Preparation of the Gifts: During this part of the Mass, which we called the "offertory" in my serving days, many things happen. The assembly sings; the ushers take up the collection; gift beaters bring the bread and wine (and other offerings) to the altar table; someone "sets the table" with the corporal (table cloth), the purificator (small towel), the Sacramentary (one of the holy books), the cup, and the basket or ciborium of bread; the presider prepares the bread and wine and says some prayers over them; the presider or deacon mixes some water with the wine; the presider says some prayers to himself; the presider washes his hands; the presider invites the assembly to pray.

They are all "preparation." That is why they call this part of the Mass "the Preparation of the Gifts."

Think of the Preparation of the Gifts as preparation for a fancy meal, Thanksgiving dinner perhaps. Obviously, your preparations for the meal are not the highlight of the day, but if you don't prepare the food and set the table, nobody eats. So it is important in this way. And as a server, you probably have more to do here than at any other part of the Mass.

For example:

- As a cross-bearer or candle-bearer, you may lead the procession of gift-bearers.

- You may need to take the wine or other gifts from the presider, after he gets them from the gift-bearers, and put them in their appropriate places.

- You may be in charge of setting the table.

- You may need to assist the presider with the wine or the washing of his hands.

- And don't forget to sing and respond to the presider's invitation to pray. You are easily seen and this will help others, especially people your own age, to sing and pray also.

Eucharistic Prayer: When Jesus took the bread in his hands, he said a Jewish prayer something like, "Blessed are You, O Lord, Our God, King of the Universe, who gave us the bread of life."

Our prayer is *much* longer and more complex, but it sill includes a long section blessing God for his wonderful gifts. In addition, you will hear:

- a retelling of the story (remember the four actions) by the presider

and a response from the
assembly that reminds us of how
Jesus died, rose from the dead,
and will return one day

- prayers for the living and the
dead

- a "Great Amen" as the people's
response (you included) to this
long prayer

- the Our Father

- an exchange of peace

The Fraction Rite: In olden times, the
Mass was called The Breaking of the Bread.
The part where this happens now is called
the Fraction Rite ("fraction," which sounds
like "fracture," means "breaking"). A good
way for this to happen is for the presider to
take a loaf of bread, perhaps baked by
someone from the parish, and break it into
little pieces that can be given to members of
the assembly. This is a very strong reminder
that each of us belongs to one body (loaf).

The pouring of the wine from one cup into
other cups which can be shared by members

of the assembly is much the same reminder.
All God's people drink from the same cup.

The Fraction Rite is also a reminder that
Jesus' body was "broken" for us and that his
blood was "poured out" for us.

The Fraction Rite is also where we say the
"Lamb of God" prayer.

Communion: This is where Christians
share the bread and wine with each other.

HOLY FOODS

Bread: If the bread you see at Mass looks more like a cracker than bread, just remember the story of the first Passover. The Israelites ate "unleavened bread" because they were in a hurry to get away from the Egyptians. Normal bread, with leaven or yeast, takes an hour or two to rise. The Israelites had no time. Centuries later, Jesus and the Apostles ate unleavened bread on the feast of the Passover as a way of remembering the freeing of their ancestors from Egypt. Centuries after Jesus, we frequently use unleavened bread at our Mass—and that's a way of remembering Jesus who was remembering Moses.

HOLY FOODS

If your church uses bread that looks and tastes like bread, enjoy. That is the way it is supposed to be. Remember: in olden times, bread was very nourishing and was sometimes all that people ate. Bread represents all food and means "life." If you share bread with your neighbors, that means you are willing to share your life with them. Sometimes, people still call wheat "the staff of life." If you look around, maybe you can find a picture of wheat somewhere in your church.

Wine: In Jesus' time, wine was an everyday drink. Like bread, it also represents all drink and all life. It is red (sometimes), like blood, and full of "spirits" that can make people lively (if they don't drink too much). On ceremonial occasions, Jewish people took a cup of wine and gave a special blessing to God.

> "Blessed are you, O Lord Our God,
> Ruler of the Universe,
> who gave us the fruit of the vine."

If you listen closely, you will hear the priest say something like this during the Preparation of the Gifts and you, along with other members of the assembly, will say, "Blessed be God forever."

At Passover, Jews and Christians say this prayer four times and drink four cups of wine. Jesus did the same thing when he celebrated Passover, including the time we call the Last Supper. We do the same as a way of remembering Jesus who was remembering his ancestors.

Fish: What? You eat no fish as Mass. Look around. You might find a fish symbol somewhere in your church. Maybe by the baptismal font. The fish is an ancient symbol of Christianity, probably because Jesus lived by a lake and ate a lot of fish. Also, the early Christians noticed that the letters of the Greek word for "fish" (IXTHUS) stood for "Jesus Christ, Son of God, Savior." Why might you find a fish by the baptismal font?

(Turn page for answer.)

Because a fish cannot live outside of water. Neither can a Christian.

Water: You will find water at the Mass, too. Just like bread and wine, water represents life too. You can live a long time without food, but only a few days without water. Look for water at the baptismal font. That is the most important place. But you will also see water used at Mass. Can you say when?

(Turn page for answer.)

During the Preparation of the Gifts, the priest mixes a little water with the wine and later washes his hands with water (just like you wash your hands before you eat—or do you?).

Remember, though, that the most important water is in the baptismal font. If the baptismal font is at the door of your church, you can bless yourself with its water as you enter. If the presider or another minister sprinkles the assembly with water—as he will do on some special feasts—you can think of the life-giving water of the baptismal water. "Holy water" is really baptismal water.

TABLE SERVICE

The altar is also a table, and as a table it has dishes, linens, and candles. The most important item is the Cup.

The Cup: The cup (sometimes called a "chalice") is the most important part of our "table setting."

In the Middle East, where Jesus came from, drinking from a common cup was a very powerful symbol. It meant you were willing to shed your blood for those who drank with you. Soldiers drank from the same cup before they want into battle. Jesus and the Apostles drank from the same cup on the night before Jesus died. That, by the way, was why Peter cut off the soldier's ear in the Garden of Gethsemane and why he felt so bad when he wound up denying Jesus three times. He had pledged to defend Jesus with his life—and he couldn't even admit he knew him!

The important thing about the cup is that we share it. Those who drink from the cup bind themselves to each other and to Jesus, the Messiah. That is why drinking from the cup is one way to receive communion.

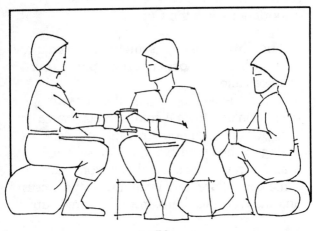

Breadplate: An old name for this is *paten*. It holds the bread that will be broken up and shared.

Breadbaskets: These hold the small or broken pieces of bread that the communion ministers give to members of the assembly. Sometimes, they are baskets. Sometimes they are ceramic or gold containers. When I was a young server, we used a container called a *ciborium* that looked very much like the chalice.

Candles: The Mass is a ceremonial meal. Just as your family might do for Thanksgiving, we set out candles. It makes the meal more special (or holy).

Tablecloth: Ceremonial meals often have a tablecloth. You might see one of these too. If there is not large tablecloth, you can find a small square piece of cloth called a "corporal" that represents a tablecloth.

Purificator: The priest uses another piece of cloth for cleaning the cup. Think of the purificator as a small towel.

Cruets: These are small pitchers that hold the wine and the water.

Flagon: If the assembly is going to share the cup, the wine might be brought up at the Preparation of the Gifts in a larger container called a "flagon."

Pitcher: Sometimes you will have a separate larger pitcher used to pour water on the hands of the priest.

Basin: This catches the water you pour on the priest's hands.

Towel: The priest uses this to dry off his hands.

HOLY BOOKS

You should be able to identify three books.

1. *The Book of the Gospels.* This book contains the Gospel reading for all the Masses of the year. This book may be decorated with special material, depending on the season or feast. A lector may carry this book high about his or her head at the entrance procession and place it upon the altar. The presider or deacon reads from it at the Gospel.

2. *The Lectionary.* This book contains all the readings for all the Masses of

the year. The lectors will read from this book.

3. *The Sacramentary.* This book contains all the other prayers and instructions for the Mass. This is the book you open for the presider.

All of these books are special (holy). Treat them with respect before, during, and after Mass. Let the people know that you know they are special. Never, for example, let them touch the ground.

HOLY FURNITURE

Do you have special furniture in your house? Perhaps a dining-room table. In some families, the dining-room table is the most expensive piece of furniture in the house, chosen with care, dusted and polished frequently, and used only on very special occasions. The furniture in your church is like this. They have probably been specially designed, just for your church. The artists who made this furniture loved working with the wood, the stone, the metals that your parish chose for this furniture. The artists did their very best work for you. And they placed it in your church so that everything seems to go together. Be sure to honor this furniture and the work that went into it, especially three pieces.

The Altar Table: This is the largest piece of furniture and is the focus of attention during the Liturgy of the Eucharist. See page 15 to see how important it is.

The Ambo, Lectern, or Pulpit: The first part of the Mass, the Liturgy of the Word, is centered here. You'll see the lector come to the ambo for the first two readings, the priest or deacon for the Gospel, and the preacher for the homily.

The Chair: This is the large chair where the presider sits.

HOLY GARMENTS

One way to show that an event or a
celebration is special is to wear special
clothing. If you are a baseball player, you
wear a uniform. If you are invited to a
wedding, you put on your best duds. If you
are graduating, you wear a gown that marks
you as a graduate. The more special the
occasion, the more special the clothes.
Sometimes clothes are so special you wear
them only at certain times. You don't wear
your football helmet to a dance; you don't go
fishing in a tuxedo.

HOLY GARMENTS

The Mass is a special occasion that requires special clothing. They even have a special name: "vestments."

For example, you may wear a *cassock* and a *surplice*. The cassock is the long garment, usually in black or red, that you put on first. The surplice is a large-sleeved half-length white garment that you put on over the cassock. Some servers wear an *alb*, a long white robe that may be hooded, tied at the waist with a *cincture* (rope belt). These are your special garments that mark you out as a minister. Make sure you get vestments that fit. And don't spoil the way they look with nasty-looking sneakers. Or even great-looking sneakers. If you are going to be seen by everyone, you and God deserve Sunday shoes that go with your special vestments.

The presider wears special garments too, of course. The important ones are:

- the alb, which many ministers, including altar servers, may wear

- the stole, a long garment worn around the neck. The priest wears at least a small stole for all of the sacraments.

HOLEY GARMENTS

- the chasuble, a large garment that can be very dramatic and beautiful. The chasuble makes the priest's gestures and blessings easier for the assembly to see. Your job is to assist the priest so that his hands are free for this work.

HOLY MOVEMENT

You can help make the Mass feel like a special moment—just by the way you move. You can also teach people—especially those your own age and younger, who look up to you—how to behave.

Sitting: Sit with your head up and back straight. Hands on your knees. Feet on the ground. Slouching, with feet stuck way out, looks ugly.

Kneeling: This may be the single hardest task for a young server, but it's important. If you fidget, cross and uncross your ankles, and keep trying to sit on your heels, everybody is going to stare. Kneel with your back straight and your head up. If it's hard, try to do it for one minute and when that's done, one minute more, and so on.

Walking: Walk with your head up and back straight—and walk more slowly than

A procession is not . . .

normal. When leading a procession, imagine
that you've just been asked to clean your
room; you'll walk at about the right speed
(just don't go the other way!). If you forget
something (like the Sacramentary), don't race
to make up, as long as you're on the way, it's
okay.

. . . a race.

Singing: Make sure you have a hymnal or songbook at your place. Use it when you're not busy with another task. Your friends, especially, will notice and will feel more comfortable singing too.

Listening: Pay attention to the lectors when they read the Scripture. You may not think anybody can tell if you're listening, but believe me, we can. And we'll be more apt to listen too is you do. (Listen, though; don't read along in a missalette.)

Holding the Book: You want to be helpful to the priest. You want to hold the book *still* and close enough to him so that he can read it easily. Priests are different, so you might ask yours how he would like you to hold the book.

Washing Hands: The washing of hands is just that, washing of hands. It's better if you pour plenty of water so that the priest's hands (but not his garments) get wet. But you need a good basin, a large towel, and a priest who likes doing things this way. You should stand in such a way that the assembly can see what you're doing.

Handshaking: One exception to the "move slowly" rule might be the handshake of

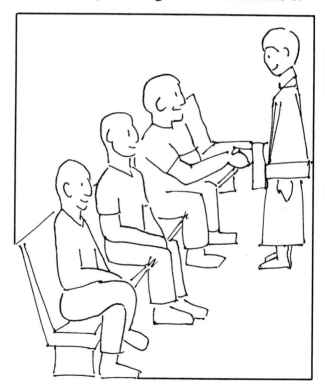

peace. If you go into the assembly to shake hands, go ahead and greet people at your normal speed. This can be a good break for you. Be sure to smile, and make sure your handshake is firm and friendly. Feel free to say more than "peace" if you meet someone you know. And it's a nice thing if you go out of your way to greet your own family.

PROCESSIONAL ITEMS

The Cross: Frequently you will act as cross-bearer, leading all the ministers and sometimes the entire assembly (on Passion Sunday, for example) in procession. You will put the cross in a prominent location. The cross is an essential element for Mass; sometimes there will be a large cross behind or above the altar, but increasingly the main cross is the one you carry in procession.

The Book of the Gospels: Often the lector or deacon will carry this in procession, holding it over his or head so that the people can see it and realize how important is the

Word of God. Or reaching the sanctuary, the book-bearer places the book in a prominent position.

Candles: Sometimes you will carry candles in the procession.

ORDER OF THE MASS

Gathering Rites

- Gathering Song and Procession
- Greetings from the Presider
- Kyrie (Lord, Have Mercy)
- Glory to God
- Opening Prayer

Liturgy of the Word

- First Reading (from Hebrew Scriptures or the Acts of the Apostles)

- Psalm Response
- Second Reading (from the letters or the Book of Revelation)
- Gospel Acclamation
- Third Reading (from the Gospels)
- Homily
- Profession of Faith
- General Intercessions

Liturgy of the Eucharist (Preparation Rites)

- Setting the table
- Procession and song
- Prayers over the bread and wine
- Mingling of water and wine
- Prayer of the priest (said softly)
- Washing of hands
- Prayer over the Gifts

Liturgy of the Eucharist (Eucharistic Prayer)

- Preface

- Holy, Holy, Holy Lord

- Consecration and story

- Memorial Acclamation (remembering Christ's death, resurrection, and second coming)

- Anamnesis (remembering)

- Intercessions and commemorations

- Great Amen

Liturgy of the Eucharist (Communion Rite)

- Lord's Prayer

- Rite of Peace

- Fraction Rite (Breaking of Bread)

- Lamb of God

- Invitation to Communion

- Sharing of Eucharist and Communion Song
- Silent Prayer or Song of Thanksgiving
- Prayer after Communion

Concluding Rites

- Final Blessing
- Dismissal
- Recession of Ministers
- Closing Song (optional)